MARRIAGE AND DIVORCE

MARRIAGE AND DIVORCE

WHAT
THE BIBLE
SAYS

James M. Efird

Wipf and Stock Publishers
EUGENE, OREGON

Wipf and Stock Publishers
199 West 8th Avenue, Suite 3
Eugene, Oregon 97401

Marriage and Divorce
What The Bible Says
By Efird, James M.
Copyright©1985 Efird, James M.
ISBN: 1-57910-675-7
Publication date: June, 2001
Previously published by Abingdon Press, 1985.

To
all those who have experienced
the joys of a real marriage
and/or
the heartbreak
of divorce

CONTENTS

*T*here are many persons to whom I owe thanks for the appearance of this little book. My appreciation goes to all those persons with whom I have counseled through the years about this sensitive topic and to many students and pastors who have indicated, and even insisted, that a work such as this would be extremely helpful in their ministry. A special word of thanks must go to James R. Mueller, an M. Div. graduate of the Duke Divinity School, who is now a Ph.D. candidate in the Graduate Department of Religion at Duke, for sharing with me his enlightening research into the many different possibilities of meaning for the Greek word translated "unchastity" in Matthew 5:32 (and 19:9).

Finally, I want to express my deepest appreciation to my dear wife, Vivian, who not only has encouraged me in the completion of this project but has typed both the rough and final copies of the manuscript. As usual I owe her a debt I cannot really repay.

It is my hope that this little book will be of some value to persons who are seeking to learn about these two important dimensions in human relationships and who sincerely want to understand what the biblical writings say about them. It is to these persons that this book is dedicated.

James M. Efird
Durham, N.C.

INTRODUCTION

*T*he institution of marriage has been a part of human society almost since the dawn of recorded history. Marriage lies at the foundation of the family unit, which supplies society with one of its chief bases for existence, continuance, and order. The moral value system of most societies is formed in and supported by the family unit. Since marriage forms the basis of the family unit, that institution has been and continues to be an integral component of almost every society.

Human beings, however, being frail and sinful entities, are not always able to make the marriage relationship work successfully. Sometimes significant breakdowns develop in relationships between husbands and wives. To deal with such situations the practice of divorce was devised as the means of escape from relationships that could range from "just bad" to deadly. This practice of divorce has also continued to be a part of almost every society "even to this day."

It may be that our present society has one of the highest divorce rates of any society ever. More than one in three first marriages end in divorce, and the percentage is growing. Couples marry with joy, hope, and promises of "till death do us part," but all too frequently they end the marriage citing "irreconcilable differences," "unfaithfulness," "incompatibility," and many more reasons. When divorce occurs, even where there is no genuinely religious basis for marriage, there are feelings of failure and guilt.

For those who stand in the Christian tradition, however, these feelings of failure and guilt are intensified, for most of these people have been taught that marriage is forever and that divorce is something no truly religious person would or could tolerate. The official or unofficial teaching of most of the various Christian churches has been: once married, always married.

Such a legalistic understanding about marriage and divorce has caused great searchings of soul, however, since many persons have found themselves in situations where a marriage relationship simply did not exist. These persons have had to wrestle with the problem of whether to remain legally married or to break the legal relationship through divorce. Many have opted for the latter course believing that to remain married under the conditions that existed was worse than divorce. That course of action, however, placed them in a situation wherein they had to deal not only with problems of failure and readjustment, and so forth, but also with inordinate feelings of guilt, since they had been taught that divorce was one of the worst offenses against God, the church, and society that could be committed.

Not only were those persons who were divorced subjected to this type of mental anguish, but they often had to fight even greater degrees of guilt if at any time they wanted to remarry. Many were told that it was bad enough to have been divorced, but if a person remarried, that was even worse. The argument was that Jesus taught that anyone who was divorced and remarried was committing adultery. Because of this understanding of Jesus' teachings some second marriages have floundered not because of the relationship between the man and the woman but because of these extreme feelings of guilt, which stood in the way of the new relationship.

We now live in an era of history when divorce and remarriage are commonplace. Hardly any family has not been touched either directly or indirectly by failure in marriage, divorce, or remarriage. To assist persons in such situations many books have been written on the topic of marriage and divorce. Most of them, however, have approached the subject from a psychological, sociological, economic, relational, or practical viewpoint. Books that are supposedly "religious" in nature have usually approached these topics from the standpoint of a theological or dogmatic perspective, that is, they discuss the topics from the standpoint that the answers are already known and thus fail to make known the basis for their ideas. Each of these types of studies has its own strengths to assist persons in learning about and coping with marriage and divorce. Most persons who are at least nominally Christian, however, want to know what the Bible teaches about these topics. There is still an authority attributed to the teachings of the Bible that transcends sociology, psychology, and even formal theology.

People who are Christians, therefore (and even those who are only nominally Christian), want to know what the Bible teaches about marriage and divorce. During the past years, as I have worked with people in the churches with regard to interpreting the Bible correctly, some of the questions asked most often have been: "What does the Bible say about marriage and divorce?" "Can a book be written that will lift out the passages dealing with these topics and interpret them as simply and nontechnically as possible?" These persons felt for varying reasons that something was needed to give some direction and instruction to persons who were wrestling with problems relating to these matters. Something was needed because on the one hand the traditional family unit and its values are being questioned and subjected to searching questions, and on the other hand there are few persons in today's society who have not been touched in some way by the breakup of a family unit. Many have experienced the trauma personally; others have seen their children or close friends involved in such situations.

Most of those persons who were asking about such a presentation were puzzled and concerned about the legalistic teaching about marriage and divorce. They had been taught by the church and its representatives that marriage is permanent, once for all, and except in quite unusual or even bizarre circumstances, divorce was not an alternative for a Christian. Certain biblical texts had been cited (and understood at face value) as absolute regulations, and no deviation could be tolerated. Part of the rationale for such a rigid understanding lay in the belief that Christians are called upon to suffer in this world, and a bad marriage is part of that suffering. Further, Christians are supposed to forgive sins against themselves; therefore, a husband's or wife's sins, no matter what, had to be ignored so that the marriage could stay intact. Couple these understandings with the idea that Christians are supposed to be meek and humble and are not to insist on their own way (even if it is right) and the definition of marriage had become rather rigid and legalistic. Any thought of divorce was, therefore, simply unthinkable, even immoral.

One can readily understand the questions that sensitive persons have had with regard to such understandings. The concern, however, was at the point of whether such an interpretation rightly reflected the biblical teachings. If so, these people seemed quite willing to live their lives by the biblical directives. Something, however, did not seem to add up. Did not the scriptural principles of forgiveness, possibility for a fresh start, concern for those in bad situations, and like motifs have any application in this area of human existence? Perhaps the time is right to ask afresh: What exactly does the Bible have to say about marriage and divorce? In an attempt to speak to precisely that question this book will focus on the understandings, teachings, and practices of marriage and divorce that are reflected in biblical times and in the biblical teachings themselves. As one approaches such a study, however, it must be understood that one has to be open to new possibilities of interpretation for texts and passages that have been understood in only one way for so long.

The procedure to be followed will be to examine the ideas connected with marriage against the background of the ancient world and its customs and presuppositions. Next, the investigation will continue with a longer section focusing on the practice of and teachings about divorce. Again these practices and teachings will be set against the backdrop of the society and culture of the biblical times.

There is one word of caution that must be mentioned with regard to some of the passages dealing with divorce. Several of these passages have textual problems associated with them, and several are subject to several possible interpretations. This means that any investigation into the possible meanings of such passages will involve some technical discussion. While some technicalities cannot be avoided, nevertheless an attempt has been made to simplify these technical discussions and to keep them to a minimum so that the nontechnical person can understand the discussion. If one wishes to enter into deeper involvement with these technicalities, the reader is referred to the concluding bibliography, which contains some good commentaries on the books in which these passages are found. Finally, there will be a short concluding essay in which I shall attempt to draw together some larger principles relating to marriage and divorce based on the biblical investigation. A few suggestions for possible ways to improve the alarming rise in the rate of divorce will be mentioned, but the primary purpose of this short study is to open up further discussion about these important topics and to give the non-scholar some insight into the biblical teachings about these two important social institutions.

To understand correctly the biblical teachings about marriage and divorce is always important, but perhaps even more so for our time and our society. Hopefully the brief expositions that follow will assist in this important task.

CHAPTER I

Marriage and Family

*E*very society, if it is to exist, continue, and survive, develops rules, regulations, and institutions for the protection of its members and for orderly progress. In almost every society the family unit has functioned as one of the chief and most basic of these societal institutions; therefore, in each society rules and guidelines have been developed for the regulation of the institution most of us designate as "marriage."

This has been done because not only does the institution of marriage and family ensure an order and stability to society in terms of preserving the traditions of the societal group but also because in human terms it usually safeguards people from arbitrary and even cruel treatment, and it provides them with some measure of security. For example, even the ancient practice of allowing men to have multiple wives (as unthinkable as this may seem to some moderns) was a way to assure women of a stable and respectable place in a society in which men quite often were in short supply.

In order to understand some of the Hebrew customs that lie at the base of Old Testament traditions about marriage and family, one must first become acquainted with certain thought patterns of the ancient world in general and the Israelite people in particular. Some of these are extremely important in interpreting the texts dealing with this important human relationship. One of the most characteristic ideas is that dealing with "corporate" thinking, that is, an emphasis upon the importance of the group rather than the wishes and well-being of the individual. The group, whether that be the family, the clan, the tribe, or the nation, was the most important element in ancient thinking. Survival was specifically tied to the well-being of the group. What was good for the group was good for the individual; what was bad for the group was to be guarded against even at the expense of an individual's life. The identity of the group, with its traditions and customs, was to be passed along from generation to generation. Central to this entire process was the family unit.

The Old Testament Teachings

Marriage in Old Testament times, therefore, has to be understood against this background, which helps one to understand some of the customs attached to that institution in Hebrew society. Many of their ways may seem curious to modern people, but their modes of operation must be understood if we hope to interpret correctly their ideas about family life. First of all, most marriages were arranged for the individuals by the families involved. This was to ensure, in part, that persons marry neither too closely nor too distantly, that is, certain marriage relationships were forbidden either because the family ties were too close (compare Gen. 20:12; Lev. 18:6-16; 20:19-21) or because the cultural and ethnic backgrounds were too distant and different (compare Gen. 24:1-4; Deut. 7:1-4; Ezra 9:1-2). Such regulations were sometimes altered in the course of Hebrew history according to the historical circumstances encountered. The important point to remember is that the survival and continuation of the group and its distinct character was the primary consideration. The leaders of the group, therefore, usually made the decision about who was to marry whom.

Not only were marriages arranged by the families, but it was considered very unusual, even unthinkable, that anyone should not be married. It is perhaps a bit of hyperbole to say that an unmarried adult was considered as a menace to the society, but it would not be far from the truth. Later Jewish tradition (found in the Talmud) taught that God becomes angry if a man is past twenty and not married! One recalls the peculiar instance in the life of Jeremiah where he was *commanded* by God not to marry. This was considered extremely unusual, but the message to be relayed by this action served to illustrate to the people of Judah just how serious their sins were and how close their destruction was (see Jer. 16:1-9). Everyone expected to be married and to be a part of a family unit. Only in unusual circumstances was this not done.

The purpose of marriage served many practical functions. Its basic function was to provide for a stable society and to serve as a major protector and transmitter of the values and traditions of the societal unit. It also provided other benefits as well. The family unit served as a means of protection for all its members, especially for women. Quite frequently in ancient times occasions arose when there were many more females than males. In such a setting females were even more vulnerable to exploitation than in normal circumstances. Thus the practice of polygyny was a part of that society. Polygyny is the technical term for a husband who has multiple wives, and while that practice seems to modern thinking exploitative and demeaning, it nevertheless served as a means of protection and security in ancient times (compare Isa. 3:18–4:1).

The fact that men were allowed to have multiple wives was, then, a part of the Old Testament scene. It was, however, as much a means of security and protection as it was exploitation of the women of that era. As the Hebrew people developed their religious understandings and practices toward the turn of the eras (that is, B.C. to A.D.), it appears that the specific trend was more in the direction of monogamy. Even so there is no *explicit* command that prohibited the practice of polygyny anywhere in the Old Testament writings. The great Jewish historian Josephus, writing in the late first century A.D., states that it "is our ancestral custom" for a man to have several wives simultaneously (*Antiquities,* xvii, 14). So that practice was still accepted as at least quasi-legitimate at the time of Jesus.

Naturally another of the primary reasons for marriage was the propogation of children. After all, the group could not survive without offspring to continue the traditions of the society, not to mention caring for the old when they were physically unable to care for themselves. So important was it to have children that a childless wife would give her handmaiden to the husband for the purpose of having offspring (compare Genesis 16, 29–30). In some later Jewish traditions, if a couple had been married for ten years and had produced no children, the man was *required* to divorce his wife and marry someone else!

Another reason for the importance given to having children was to ensure the continuation of the family line. That was important, first, so that property could be passed along and retained, because the land was viewed as a gift of God given as a trust to the Israelite people. The land must be carefully preserved and passed along. Second, the people of the ancient world did not have the same kind of belief in life after death as later generations came to know. In those times, whenever a person died, that "person" went to the place of the dead called Sheol. This was not a place of reward or punishment, and all people went there at death. It was viewed as a place of dim and shadowy existence, the weakest kind of "life" one can imagine.

Because of the Hebrew emphasis upon "corporate" personality, all generations, past and future, however, were present in the persons currently alive. Therefore, to have a direct link with the land of the living through physical offspring somehow made the gloomy existence in Sheol less oppressive. It was considered absolutely necessary, therefore, for the husband to have physical descendants.

This was considered such an important matter that a law was devised to ensure the continuation of the family line. This law is usually designated as the "levirate" law, from the Latin word *levir*, meaning brother-in-law. Simply put, if a husband died leaving no children, it became the duty of the next of kin (preferably a brother of the deceased) to "visit" the widow for the purpose of impregnating her. If a brother were not available, any near kinsman of the husband could perform the duty. This is sometimes referred to as "levirate marriage," but marriage did not always take place after the widow became pregnant. If it did, the woman usually became another wife of the deceased husband's kinsman. Whatever happened, however, the first child born was considered to be the child of the deceased for purposes of inheritance and the longed-for link to the land of the living. Any other children, if the two were then married, were considered the children of the living husband (compare Genesis 38; Ruth 3–4; Deut. 25:5-10).

Perhaps a brief explanation of the lines of authority that were followed in ancient practices of marriage and family would be helpful for our larger discussion. In the ancient world there were basically two types of marriage/family relationships. One centered in the authority of the female, usually designated matriarchal. Here the male left his own people and became a part of the wife's family. A variation on this procedure is reflected in the practice of a man marrying a woman who continued to live with her people while the husband only made periodic visits to his wife. There are vestiges of this latter practice in the Old Testament, most notably in the story of Samson (see Judg. 15:1).

The second type is usually designated "patriarchal" and is the usual form found in the Old Testament literature. Here the male was considered the authority figure in the family unit. His power was not totally absolute but nearly so. As already noted he made arrangements for the marriage of the children, directed the family's movements, and served as a type of judge over disputes within the family unit. It was indeed basically a male-oriented and male-dominated society. Most ancient societies were, and Hebrew society certainly was.

Partly because of this societal structure, only the husband (in Hebrew practice) had the authority to divorce his wife. The wife had no such recourse. There were instances in practice, however, where the wife could have pressure brought to bear upon the husband to give her a divorce if she wanted it. The husband did, after all, have responsibilities and duties toward and for his wife and was expected to fulfill them. If not, he was expected to divorce his wife and make some kind of restitution to her.

The institution of marriage in ancient Israel, therefore, served multiple purposes. It assured a certain stability to the societal unit and was the primary means for passing along the values and traditions of the group. It served as a means for the protection of the members of the group, especially the women. Further it served as the means of expression for and a means to guard against abuse of human sexuality.

The Hebrew people understood and interpreted human sexuality as a positive gift from God. There is no concept of the later Greek dualism between spirit and matter where anything that had to do with "fleshly" activities was considered evil and inferior. Such thinking led to the idea that since the sex act itself is outwardly, at least, physical, sexuality was evil and to be shunned if possible. The Hebrews knew nothing of such thinking. For them the sex act was beautiful and to be enjoyed to the fullest. A marriage was a time of great festivity, partly because it signified the beginning of sexual activity on the part of the man and woman. The newly bethrothed man was even excused from participating in war (compare Deut. 20:7)!

This simply demonstrates that human sexuality was taken very seriously by the ancient Hebrews. It was a source of good because it was pleasurable to the persons involved and because it was the means whereby the new generations came into being.

Perhaps the classic example of the exaltation of human sexuality is found in the Song of Songs. This book has been an embarrassment at times to Jews and Christians alike. Some interpreters have argued that the book should be understood as an allegory symbolizing the love of God for Israel or the love of Christ for the church. This writing is not an allegory, however. It is a declaration of the joys of human sexuality, and certain traditions even suggest that portions of this book were sung during the wedding processional and during the time of the wedding feast.

While the Hebrew people did rejoice in the joys of sexual activity, there was also the understanding that this gift of God could be and often was abused. They saw this all around in the ancient world, especially when they came into the land of Canaan where people worshiped Baal. Associated with the worship of Baal was the practice of sacred prostitution, and the evils and excesses of this cult were abhorrent to the Hebrews. In addition to religious promiscuity was the natural tendency of the human creature to take beautiful things and debase them. Such was true, perhaps especially so, of sexuality as well. These people believed that sexual activity must be set within a "proper" context. That context was one of long-term commitment and loyalty, which was located primarily within the setting of marriage and family. Therefore, one finds many laws dealing with the regulation of this activity in Old Testament society.

Several illustrations may help in understanding their great concern for proper sexual practice. One of the most elemental regulations in this area was concerned with what today could be called modesty. One's "private parts" were not to be revealed in public or in private, except in the most unusual of circumstances. Further, there were strict prohibitions against incest (Lev. 18:6-18; 20:11-12, 14, 20; Deut. 27:20, 22), bestiality (Lev. 18:23; 20:15-16), homosexuality (Lev. 18:22; 20:13), and various and sundry sexual "irregularities" (compare Exod. 22:16; Lev. 19:20, 29; 15:24; 18:19; 20:18; Deut. 25:11; etc.). It was also considered extremely important for the wife to have been a virgin upon the occasion of the wedding. Obviously there was some form of evidence used to validate this fact, such as a blood-stained garment (see Deut. 22:13-21). This "proof" was important in that society because a man could put aside his wife, if he so wished, without any responsibility on his part, by charging that she was not a virgin when he married her. This "proof" was a protection for the woman against petty and arbitrary accusations by the husband. In other words, human sexuality, this beautiful gift of God, was subject to abuse and perversion. The Hebrew people, therefore, believed that such a marvelous gift should be guarded from the unbridled sinfulness of human nature. Thus stringent regulations were adopted to retain the high dignity that they felt should be afforded to this aspect of humanity.

Marriage and family, therefore, was a major element in Hebrew society. Its purposes were many: to ensure stability in the social order; to procreate so that the people could continue; to teach the children the value system of the society (compare Exod. 12:26; Josh. 4:1-7); to ensure the orderly transition of property and possessions; to guard against the exploitation of women; to give proper expression to human sexuality; to guard against sexual misconduct. In short, marriage was one of the key stabilizing and humanizing practices among all the institutions of Israel. There were many ideals associated with the institution of marriage that were not always upheld. There were two reasons for that failure: (1) the natural sinfulness of human beings who want to bend the regulations to suit themselves; and (2) the problems caused by living in a less-than-perfect world. Nevertheless, the institution of marriage was held in high esteem, and the ideal was at least preserved and hoped for even though not exactly realized.

It is usually agreed that the ultimate ideal for marriage and family found in the Old Testament teachings is monogamy—one man and one woman married for life. This appears to be the intent of the teaching in Genesis 2:24: "Therefore a man leaves his father and his mother and cleaves to his wife, and they become one flesh." As already indicated, polygamy was never officially forbidden in the Old Testament documents, but the teaching especially as the centuries went by was more and more toward the ideal of one husband and one wife. Even though historical circumstances sometimes made this ideal practically impossible and even though human depravity frequently cheapened sexual activity, the ideal was never forgotten.

The New Testament Teachings

One finds in the New Testament much the same understanding in terms of emphasis and principles for marriage as that found in the Old Testament. Marriage is basically a means of stability and order in society; it is the means whereby the values and traditions of the people were passed along; it was understood as the means given to humankind for the regulation and proper practice of human sexuality (compare I Cor. 7:2-9, 36). There do seem to be certain shifts of emphasis, however, for now the basic criterion is that of *monogamy alone* and the traditions to be passed along to children are no longer both national/ethnic and religious but primarily, if not exclusively, religious. Christianity was understood to be universalistic (for all people), not primarily limited to one group. Further, with the emphasis upon monogamy, more attention began to be paid to relationship per se than in Old Testament times.

The basic definition of marriage for the New Testament appears to be rooted in the teaching given by Jesus in Mark 10:7-8: "For this reason a man shall leave his father and mother and be joined to his wife, and the two shall become one flesh. So they are no longer two but one flesh." Most persons who study this episode (10:1-9) are preoccupied with the question of divorce (as were the religious leaders who were attempting to entrap Jesus), but Jesus turns the question away from divorce to a discussion of marriage and what ideally marriage should be. Real marriage occurs where two people become one. If such a union takes place, then there can be no divorce, for by definition a single entity is not divisible (except perhaps by outsiders).

Paul closely follows this teaching when he argues in I Corinthians 7:3-4 that each person in the marriage covenant surrenders to the other control over his or her very being. "The husband should give to his wife her conjugal rights, and likewise the wife to her husband. For the wife does not rule over her own body, but the husband does; likewise the husband does not rule over his own body, but the wife does." In such an understanding there is the same idea that Jesus enunciated in Mark 10:7-8, and where such a relationship exists there can be no divorce. Further, contrary to what some have been led to believe, Paul does not in any way depreciate the institution of marriage as a somewhat lower life-style than the nonmarried state. Many have interpreted Paul wrongly at this point, because they fail to recognize that Paul is speaking to a specific situation in I Corinthians 7.

The people in Corinth had asked Paul basically two questions relating to marriage and sexuality. The reason for their questions was an understanding in certain Greek thought patterns that anything that had to do with the physical aspects of life was evil. Since the sex act is, externally at least, physiological, the reasoning was that sexual activity is inherently evil. This type of thinking was prevalent in many parts of the Greco-Roman world and caused no little discussion among the people in the church at Corinth. Some were arguing that people who were not married should remain single (and supposedly celibate) and that those who were married refrain from sexual activity.

Paul responded that it was quite right and proper for married persons to engage in sexual activity. He even indicated that it was mandatory, "lest you be tempted." As for those who were not married he argued that there was no sin in marrying. In fact, marriage is the proper outlet and context for sexual activity; therefore, Paul urged marriage rather than promiscuity.

As a general principle, however, Paul counseled those who were unmarried not to marry. His reason for this advice was very practical, not theoretical or dogmatic. Paul believed, along with most of the early Christians, that Jesus was to return very soon, within their lifetime. When the return (called technically the *Parousia*) occurred, it was thought that there would be a period of intense persecution directed against the people of God. In such a situation no one needs any more duties or responsibilities than absolutely necessary. Marriage entails responsibilities and obligations that could be burdensome during such a time. And further, one would not wish to have small children who would have to suffer through those difficult moments. Paul's counsel to those who were unmarried, therefore, does not reflect a negative outlook toward marriage or sexuality, because his advice was predicated solely on a practical basis, not on theological negativity toward these matters.

In fact Paul believed that marriage is one of those stabilizing institutions for society in general and particularly the church community. This is clearly taught in Colossians, where Paul acknowledges several societal structures and comments upon the lines of authority current and accepted in his time and place. The husband-wife relationship was one of those. In that time it was accepted that the husband was the authority figure in the family unit. He was trained for that purpose, and it was his responsibility to look after his family. Responsibility and authority must somehow be connected. The wife, however, also had duties and responsibilities and a certain amount of authority as well. One should be careful to understand that Paul is speaking in such a setting about accepted authority *in his time*, not that he is laying down societal absolutes for all eras to come. His basic principles are that the husband and wife fulfill their designated responsibilities. The fact that they are Christians in whatever societal structure lifts their relationship to a higher level than the normal practices of the world (compare Col. 3:18–4:1).

The marriage relationship was held in high regard in the early church. For example, the author of

Ephesians (an admirer of Paul) used that very relationship as an analogy of the relationship between Christ and the church (compare Eph. 5:21-33). Again, cultural understandings of that day are involved in the figure (that is, the husband is the higher authority), but it is the relational aspect that stands at the center of this discussion. In marriage there is a covenant made that commits each party to the other, thereby establishing a relationship in which each contributes to the other's well-being. The passage from Genesis that Jesus cited is used by the author of Ephesians to emphasize a "mystery." The mystery involves understanding how two people can become one while yet remaining two; how two people can become so much a part of each other that they can be one while at the same time having their own individual identities sharpened and fulfilled. The author applies this mystery to the church—how the members of the church can be one with Christ and yet remain individuals and have that individuality increased and sharpened not only for one's own development but more importantly for the development of the church and its members. To use such an analogy for the relation between Christ and the church indicates the high esteem marriage commanded, at least in theory.

In the New Testament, then, the emphasis in marriage had been strongly drawn toward monogamy under the influence of Jesus' teaching. Paul appears to have known that teaching as did the author of the Epistle to the Ephesians. This emphasis is perhaps also reflected in the literature that represents the thinking of the church toward the conclusion of the first century A.D. One finds in I Timothy a passage that sets forth guidelines for persons who hold office in the church. One of these is that an overseer (bishop) or deacon be "the husband of one wife" (I Tim. 3:2, 12). Many have interpreted this restriction as directed against divorced persons who had remarried.

It is possible that such a meaning was intended, but it is also possible that it was directed against the practice of having more than one wife *at a time*. Many commentators believe that the original intent of this directive was aimed at polygamy. If one wishes to be absolutely literalistic about the saying, it would then mean that even a person who had been widowed and had remarried could not be considered eligible. Such a meaning is very unlikely given the high mortality rate among young women who had babies in those days. Whatever one wishes to think about the exact meaning of this passage, it is certain that a clean and wholesome family life was expected of the church's leaders.

There are several other passages that touch upon the general subject of marriage, but these are either cited as figures of speech to illustrate another point (compare for example Rom. 7:1-3) or basically follow the general teachings of Colossians and Ephesians for family life (compare I Pet. 3:1-7). Marriage was considered so beautiful that the author of Revelation, as of Ephesians, used the figure to depict the union between Christ and the people of the church (compare Rev. 21:2, 9).

In summary, then, marriage as it is understood, depicted, and practiced among the biblical peoples served numerous positive purposes. This institution served as the primary stabilizing component in early Hebrew society and retained that important function during the period when Israel was a nation and later in exile. Christians understood marriage in much the same way as a significant aspect of society. The family was the primary instrument for preserving and transmitting the fundamental value system of the people of God, which had tremendous importance for the social practices of the larger community. Marriage served as a means for the expression and practice of human sexuality and as a means for guarding against the natural human inclination toward abuse and even perversion of this beautiful gift fom God. The institution of marriage served to protect individuals from exploitation in the midst of a world that was (and still is) cruel and unfeeling. In both the Old and New Testaments marriage was held in such high esteem that it was used to draw analogies for the relationship between God and God's people (compare Hos. 1–3; as well as Eph. 5:21-33). In fact it may not be far from correct to say that as far as the biblical writers were concerned, the marriage relationship was the most important relationship a human being could have, next to one's relationship with God, of course. The author of Hebrews perhaps

said it best: "Let marriage be held in honor among all
. . ." Heb. 13:4a).

The ideal for marriage was held to be one man and
one woman together for life. Practically, the biblical
writers understood that the world in which we live is
not the best of all possible worlds, nor do we live in
the Kingdom of God, that ideal state where everyone
is and does as one is supposed to be and to do.
Because of this recognition there are certain teachings in the biblical materials that deal with divorce,
the breaking of the marriage covenant and tie. To
that discussion we now turn.

CHAPTER II

Divorce

*T*he ideas and principles related to marriage in the biblical materials have been discussed in rather general terms, partly because there is usually very little disagreement about the teachings relating to that significant institution. It is somewhat different with divorce, however, because divorce is an extremely serious action, which legally dissolves the marriage bond between a man and a woman. Since that action was of such consequence, both societally and individualistically, specific regulations were devised by the community to ensure fairness and some semblance of order to this negative and destructive action. Some of the biblical teachings about divorce are clear and almost certain to be understood correctly. Others, however, are less than completely clear when only a simple and superficial reading of the text is undertaken. Therefore, in this discussion about divorce there will be more detailed analysis of the biblical texts that speak to that subject.

In order to prepare for such an analysis one must first become acquainted with certain principles, which underlie a proper approach to the interpretation of the Scriptures. One must always keep in mind that the texts under examination have a history and a context, and that history and context must be pursued and understood (as much as possible) in order to interpret the individual texts properly. Further, one must be aware of the literary styles and types that were used by the biblical writers in order to present their ideas and teachings.

For example, with regard to the teachings of Jesus, not simply about divorce but generally, one must realize that Jesus was a wisdom teacher and used wisdom methodology in his teaching. Wisdom teaching basically consisted of figures of speech, usually taken from everyday life, frequently coupled with the Hebrew tendency toward hyperbole (exaggeration). These teachings took the form of proverbs, riddles, parables, allegories, and the like. They made a point and challenged the hearer to make a comparison between the point of the teaching and one's own life and practice. For example, Jesus said: "If your right eye causes you to sin, pluck it out and throw it away; . . . And if your right hand causes you to sin, cut it off and throw it away; . . . " (Matt. 5:29-30). In another passage Jesus told a rich young man, ". . . go, sell what you have, and give to the poor . . . " (Mark 10:21; compare also Luke 18:22). It is obvious that very few, if any (except for mentally deranged persons), take these sayings literally. To be sure, they were not intended to be understood literally! Rather they are examples of wisdom type teaching with a large dash of hyperbole. There is a point to be understood from the teachings, but the point is a principle or guideline, not an absolute law to be followed exactly for all times and all places.

As the appropriate passages on divorce are examined, background, setting, and type of teaching will assist the interpreter in understanding the original intent and purpose of the sayings. These elements will be mentioned as each passage is examined.

The Old Testament Passages

When one comes to the collection of books known as the Old Testament, one finds that divorce was an accepted but not encouraged practice in Hebrew society. The basic teaching that speaks to the problem is usually understood to be Deuteronomy 24:1ff.: "When a man takes a wife and marries her, if then she finds no favor in his eyes because he has found some indecency in her, and he writes her a bill of divorce and puts it in her hand and sends her out of his house. . . ." This particular saying was, in all probability, originally part of a directive regarding the possible remarriage with a wife whom a former husband had previously divorced. This passage, however, came to have more significance than that, for it appears that here is a direct allusion to the legal basis for divorce in Hebrew society with the attendant requirement that the divorced wife be given a written document to verify the dissolution of the marriage.

As discussed above, the husband was the authority in the family unit. Therefore, in Hebrew society only the husband had the right of divorce. It was believed that to divorce a wife, however, there must be some legitimate grounds for this action. That basis is given in the phrase "some indecency." The term is probably ambiguous by design and means something other than adultery since the penalty for adultery was not divorce but death by stoning for both the wife and her lover. This passage (and this specific term) later served as the focus for discussion about divorce when specific reasons were set down in order to regulate the practice.

There are few passages in the Old Testament writings until the postexilic period that deal with divorce. That divorce was permissible and a part of the accepted practice of the societal community was assumed by the Old Testament writers. One finds a few illustrations drawn from the practice of divorce in certain texts. The practice of giving the wife a "decree of divorce" is used figuratively in Jeremiah 3:8 to illustrate the break between God and the people of Judah. And there could be in Hosea (compare Hosea 1:9b) a pattern for the written bill of divorce, which the husband was obliged to give to the wife. This written statement was probably an attempt to protect a woman who had been divorced from the charge of adultery if she later became the wife of some other man or was engaged in sexual liaison though not remarried.

It is in the postexilic period (that is, after 538 B.C.) that most discussion about divorce is found in the Old Testament literature. As the biblical student knows, the Judean (southern) kingdom fell to the Babylonians in 586 B.C. Jerusalem was burned, and most of the people were carried off into exile in Babylonia. In 539 Cyrus and the Persians defeated the Babylonian Empire and allowed the exiled peoples kept there to return to their homelands. They also encouraged them to worship their gods once more. In 538 a contingent of Jewish people from Babylon returned to Judea and found a dismal scene. The area was largely still in ruins; most of the land that was of any value had been taken by other peoples; and the new community had no real economic base. For many years the community struggled to exist, living on the verge of being assimilated and absorbed into the surrounding peoples.

In this setting many Jewish men began to divorce their Jewish wives to be able to marry women from the families of the surrounding peoples. This was a very pragmatic course of action because these families would have connections and resources so as to aid the Jewish community in its struggle for survival. It was also a very selfish mode of behavior! Into this setting a prophet, known today as Malachi, came. He spoke out against this particular practice of divorce because he feared that such actions could destroy the traditions and identity of the Jewish people. Thus he argued that marriage was a covenant that should be honored and should not be broken simply for expedient reasons. Here is the text of Malachi 2:13-16:

> [13]And this again you do. You cover the Lord's altar with tears, with weeping and groaning because he no longer regards the offering or accepts it with favor at your hand. [14]You ask, "Why does he not?" Because the Lord was witness to the covenant between you and the wife of your youth, to whom you have been faithless, though she is your companion and your wife by covenant. [15]Has not the one God made and sustained for us the spirit of Life? And what does he desire? Godly offspring. So take heed to yourselves, and let none be faithless to the wife of his youth. [16]"For I hate divorce, says the Lord the God of Isarel, and covering one's garment with violence, says the Lord of hosts. So take heed to yourselves and do not be faithless."

One notes that Malachi does not indicate that divorce *per se* is evil or wrong. The circumstances and reasons for divorce *in this historical context* were not valid according to his understanding. His concern was that in this mixture of cultures and peoples the unique traditions and value system of the Hebrew people would be lost. There is no indication here that divorce was now done away, nor was this passage understood in later Jewish thinking as an absolute prohibition against divorce. And, understood in its context it is not.

The tendency to absolutize isolated biblical teachings into legalisms is strong among some interpreters, and such persons like to use the Malachi passage to argue for the idea that by the time of that prophet God's revelation was clear that no divorce was allowable. It is interesting to note that most students of the Old Testament date the teachings of Malachi somewhere between 520 and 450 B.C. One notes with interest, however, that during the careers of Nehemiah (444-432 B.C.) and Ezra (400 B.C.), the historical situation had changed somewhat, and a different teaching was formulated. What was it and why was it presented?

When Nehemiah and Ezra appeared on the scene in Judah, they found that the Jewish people were frequently marrying persons from the surrounding peoples. To their mind such a practice threatened the integrity of the Jewish traditions and the uniqueness of the Hebrew religious faith. To counter this threat both of these leaders commanded the people to refrain from marrying foreigners, and Ezra even commanded them to divorce their foreign spouses and send them away, them and any children born of the union (compare Ezra 9:1-2; 10; and Neh. 10:30; 13:23-25)! Here divorce was not condemned; it was required.

Such actions may seem rather harsh and even cruel to modern thinking. If one places oneself in the historical situation that existed at the time of Ezra, the reasons behind such a course become understandable if not acceptable. The Jewish community was weak and powerless, subject to the whims of the peoples surrounding it. In order to survive, and survival was exactly what was at stake here, the leaders felt that extreme measures were necessary to preserve the integrity and uniqueness of this group. These were desperate times, and the desperate times called for extreme measures, which may not have been acceptable under "normal" circumstances, such as the requirement of divorce noted under Nehemiah and Ezra.

It is clear from an investigation of these passages that divorce as an accepted social custom was clearly a part of the Hebrew community in Old Testament times, both in the preexilic and postexilic eras. Divorce was considered a serious matter, however, so that regulations were devised to ensure that the practice of divorce was not abused. In later times, for example, it became part of the betrothal agreement that a payment of some agreed upon amount was to be given to the wife if the husband divorced her. In the history of the Hebrew community there were times when the practice of divorce was frowned upon (as with Malachi) and other times when the act of divorce was demanded (as with Ezra). In all times, however, the institution of marriage and family was considered to be the key to holding together the moral structure and traditional integrity of the society at large. Divorce was part of that society and was never wholly forbidden in ancient times, but the practice was not so widespread as to cause instability in the society (except perhaps in the time of Malachi).

After the Torah was accepted as authoritative for the Jewish people (about 400 B.C.), it became necessary to interpret that Scripture properly. Thus there emerged a group of people whose basic purpose was to study and interpret the Law. These persons have been popularly known as Rabbis, though in these early days many of them were leaders of "schools" of interpretation much like the Wisdom teachers. At the time when Jesus appeared on the scene there were two very famous and well-known schools: the school of Hillel and the school of Shammai. These two debated many matters of interpretation in the Torah. One of the areas of debate centered on the problem of divorce.

The Hillel group tended to be more flexible in its interpretation of the Torah and granted wide range in the understanding and application of the old directives. With regard to the passage in Deuteronomy 24:1 and the mention of "some indecency," this school understood that phrase to include anything from a wife's serving a meal that the husband did not like to becoming old and less attractive to the husband than younger women. The Shammai group, however, was much more strict in its interpretations and held that in the case of divorce sexual misconduct was the only legitimate cause for which a wife could be put away. One can surmise by the intensity of the debate and the many possible interpretations that were suggested, especially by the Hillel school, that this issue must have been a problem in that period of Jewish history. Some have even argued that the diversity in the definition of "some indecency" indicates that divorce was being enacted (for the flimsiest of reasons), perhaps causing the problem to escalate to scandalous proportions.

There is one other historical item that the interpreter should keep in mind when attempting to understand the New Testament teachings about divorce. This concerns the problem of the somewhat questionable marriage of Herodias to Herod Antipas. Antipas ruled (with Rome's support) over Galilee, where Jesus lived, and Perea (a small strip of territory on the east side of the Jordan River). Herodias had been married to Herod's half brother, Philip. Herod divorced his wife and persuaded Herodias to come live with him. Many think that she did this without proper legal status, not having been officially divorced from her husband, Philip. Even if the separation had been legal, however, the law said that one could not have his brother's wife (Lev. 18:16; 20:21). John the Baptizer spoke out against this situation rather strongly and ultimately lost his life over his public outcry regarding this scandal. It is possible that this incident may have left its mark on certain of Jesus' teachings as well.

With this all-too-brief summary of some of the ideas about divorce current at the time of Jesus and the New Testament church, the time has come to examine the specific passages that touch upon this subject.

The New Testament Passages

Mark 10:2-9: [2]And Pharisees came up and in order to test him asked, "Is it lawful for a man to divorce his wife?" [3]He answered them, "What did Moses command you?" [4]They said, "Moses allowed a man to write a certificate of divorce, and to put her away." [5]But Jesus said to them, "For your hardness of heart he wrote you this commandment. [6]But from the beginning of creation, 'God made them male and female.' [7]For this reason a man shall leave his father and mother and be joined to his wife, [8]and the two shall become one flesh.' So they are no longer two but one flesh. [9]What therefore God has joined together, let not man put asunder."

This passage has been one used prominently in discussions about marriage and divorce within the Christian community through the centuries. As it stands in the flow of Mark's Gospel, it is one in a series of questions put to Jesus by the Jewish religious authorities in order to "entrap" him. It is quite probable that behind this question in the historical context of those times lay the debate that was going on between certain Rabbinic schools whose purpose it was to attempt to interpret the Torah properly. As already noted (Deut. 24:1), the Scripture allowed for divorce for "some indecency," but the problem lay in what such an "indecency" might be. By posing this question to Jesus the religious authorities may have felt that no matter what answer Jesus gave he would alienate some persons. And further, if Jesus had given some radically new teaching, this could have been used in some way against him. As Mark presents the story this appears to be his understanding of this questioning with regard to the motivation of the religious authorities (compare also Mark 12:13ff., 18ff., and perhaps 28ff.).

Here one sees that the basic question was whether a husband could divorce his wife. Jesus replied, in typical Wisdom type methodology, by asking them a question, namely what the Scriptures taught. They replied that Moses had allowed for divorce as long as a husband gave to the woman a certificate of divorce. Whereupon Jesus, also appealing to the Scripture, made the point that preoccupation with divorce is out of line with God's intentions for human relationships. He cited the Genesis passage, which he interpreted as one man and one woman becoming one. The two actually are to become one personality, and by definition, where this occurs, there can be no possibility for divorce. Where that occurs, God has indeed joined the two together.

The response by Jesus does not really speak to the issue of divorce, but it (as Jesus so often does) goes to the heart of the real issue. The real issue is not to be preoccupied with how one may legally slip out of a marriage but rather how one makes a real marriage. The definition Jesus gives is a beautiful one, an ideal, perhaps salted with a bit of his Wisdom hyperbole. It is clear, however, that Jesus viewed marriage as one of if not the highest of human relationships. This relationship holds many positive possibilities for both individuals and the well-being of society. Such a relationship should not be entered casually but very seriously, and such an important relationship should not be terminated simply by "whim" or "fancy." Two people becoming one is a definition of marriage that far exceeds the legal requirements of the law.

Clearly where such a relationship is established there cannot be any possibility for divorce. It is interesting then to note the last comment of Jesus in this setting, "what God has joined together, let not man put asunder." Here the word for "man" is not the same as that used in Mark 10:2, where the word means "husband." Jesus, again probably using hyperbole, charges the human race to be more attentive to the real purpose of marriage and hold the institution of marriage in high regard. (It is also possible that the teaching here could even refer to a third party, but that is not likely.)

This passage, therefore, should be understood against the setting of the times and the setting in the life of Jesus. One cannot fail to note that Jesus never says that the old law had been declared null and void. He seems rather to accept it as part of the teaching of the Scriptures, but he wishes to call attention to the unique place of this institution in God's plan for the world. The teaching is not, therefore, an *absolute* teaching about divorce, but a description of what real marriage is supposed to be. The emphasis is shifted from a preoccupation with divorce to an emphasis on marriage. Jesus wanted to turn their attention from self-centered manipulation of human relationships and of playing games with the law to an understanding of what real marriage is supposed to be.

The major emphasis here, however, appears to be Jesus' implicit and strong understanding that marriage is supposed to be monogamous. Jesus' teaching makes it quite clear that "one and one equal one." There seems to be no room under this definition for multiple wives (or husbands). How could three people have such a relationship? This type of understanding and emphasis would naturally lead to a more egalitarian relationship, especially as women were seen to be more equal partners than understood before. As mentioned above (cf. pp. 29-30) this strong emphasis by Jesus on monogamy was understood and upheld by Paul and others in the early church.

To this episode and significant teaching of Jesus Mark has added another.

> *Mark 10:10-12:* [10]And in the house the disciples asked him again about this matter. [11]And he said to them, "Whoever divorces his wife and marries another, commits adultery against her; [12]and if she divorces her husband and marries another, she commits adultery."

This passage appears rather innocent and straightforward to modern minds, partly because the idea of equality within marriage is much more acceptable now than it was then. Close examination of the saying, however, reveals some very interesting and unusual interpretative problems. First of all, there is the curious idea that a man could commit adultery against his wife. This was not a part of the culture and tradition of the Jewish people at that time. The question, therefore, arises as to what was intended by this teaching. It is entirely possible that Jesus was teaching something radically new, the natural consequence of the emphasis on monogamy, but one notes that the revolutionary character of the teaching is not mentioned at all. Mark says, however, that the disciples asked Jesus about the matter privately, which would explain why there was no uproar about what would have been seen as a changing of the law.

The second item of interest lies in the teaching that assumes that a wife could divorce her husband. This action was simply not an option for Jewish wives in that time. Again, either Jesus is giving some radically new teaching (to which there is no unusual reaction) or else there may be different ways to understand the saying. One of the most usual interpretations among scholars is that the early church took the teachings of Jesus not as absolute legalisms but as guidelines and felt perfectly free to apply those guidelines to new settings, or even to create new teachings to fit their new situations. In the Greco-Roman world the wife did have the right to divorce her husband, and Mark's Gospel was written in the midst of a Gentile community, that is, Rome. Many scholars feel that the teaching was reapplied to speak to a situation and problem encountered in a different culture with different procedures under the law for wives. It is interesting to note that the early church did not think that such reinterpretations of the text were illegitimate nor contrary to Jesus' intention. This could be one explanation of this teaching.

There is yet another dimension to be considered, however, in the interpretation of this passage. In the original Greek text there is a problem in that according to the early copies of Mark there are three possible wordings of the passage. The usual translations with which we are familiar have chosen only one of the possibilities, but other alternatives are possible, even probable. Two of the texts give essentially the same translation as that given by the Revised Standard Version. The other, however, is quite different. It reads, "If a woman [wife] should leave a husband and marry another, she is commiting adultery." In other words the saying here in verse 12 would refer to a wife who left her husband and married someone else without *benefit of divorce*. If this is the correct reading, then the question is not about whether divorce is acceptable or not; the point would be that living with or marrying someone else without having been divorced constitutes adultery. Many of the best commentaries on Mark's Gospel argue that this reading is probably the one closest to the original reading.

If this understanding of the saying is correct (that is, "If a woman should leave [but not properly divorce] a husband and marry another . . ."), the question then can be asked: What could possibly have been the original setting for such a teaching in Jesus' time? There does happen to be a possible explanation. As noted above it was a matter of some discussion during that period that Herodias (who was the wife of Philip, one of Herod the Great's sons) had left her husband and married Herod Antipas, the ruler over Galilee where Jesus lived (and who also was a son of Herod the Great). It is probable from the evidence available that this switch was made without a legal divorce. This incident was, therefore, considered scandalous in that time, and it is well known that John the Baptizer spoke out quite strongly against the situation—ultimately bringing about his execution.

The teaching originally may have been directed, therefore, toward a wife's leaving her husband to go live as a wife with another man without the proper legal and social directives being fulfilled. The teaching may well reflect this specific historical problem of the scandal of Herod and Herodias. In the setting of the early church then, especially in the Gentile world, this saying would naturally have been applied both to husbands as well as wives.[1]

---

[1]One may legitimately ask how and why the saying in Mark came to be altered. This probably occurred in the process of the transmission of the text to make this passage conform to similar teachings found in other Gospels. In text-critical circles this phenomenon is known as "harmonization," that is, making the Gospel accounts read exactly alike. When such a change took place, some texts would read as the older text had, and some would reflect the alteration. Some even would show signs of an attempt to make one saying from the two. The process by which interpreters attempt to unravel what happened is often quite tedious and detailed, but such investigation must be done if the original meanings and intent are to be uncovered in the study of biblical materials.

What one finds in this passage, therefore, is a saying that originally had reference to a specific event, that is, Herodias' leaving her husband and without proper legal proceedings living as the wife of Herod Antipas. Such action was considered absolutely scandalous in those days. The saying did not originally have any direct connection with the morality (or lack thereof) with regard to divorce *per se*. As the saying was used by the early church, the teaching and principle were applied to both husbands and wives, partly at least because of Jesus' emphasis on monogamy. The confusion in this passage has arisen because of the textual problem. Mark placed this saying immediately after the longer saying about marriage because it was similar in subject matter and because it illustrated the point that marriage was of great significance and was not to be treated in a cavalier manner.

Summary

What then can be learned from an examination of these two passages in Mark's Gospel? The most important point is that which emphasizes the importance of and the intention of God for marriage. Marriage is a very significant human institution, which must never be taken lightly. The ideal is for one man and one woman to be united in such a way that they become one. Where that occurs *there can be no divorce*. By definition the two have become inseparable. This is the ideal, the way God intended marriage to be according to Jesus. There is an emphasis upon monogamy and unity.

What do the passages have to say about divorce? Some have argued that these passages are legalistic commands that deny the possibility of divorce under any circumstances. Some even call this teaching a "dominical saying" (that is, an absolute teaching by Jesus) with regard to this matter. Upon closer examination of the text, however, one finds that Jesus never says that the old law of Moses was no longer valid. He only responded to the question by explaining why Moses had allowed this practice, that is, because of human nature and the human condition of sinfulness. He did not reject the possibility for divorce except as he gave a definition of what marriage ought to be and what God intended it to be.

In the second passage the teaching is not as clear because of the textual problem. It appears, however, that Jesus here is talking more about spouses abandoning their mates than he is talking about divorce *per se*. The teaching seems to be rooted in his idea that marriage should be between one man and one woman. If either deserts the other to live with someone else without proper legal procedures, that is an adulterous situation. This passage may not have been originally directed toward divorce but rather proper procedures for divorce and remarriage.

Matthew 5:31-32: ³¹"It was also said, 'Whoever divorces his wife, let him give her a certificate of divorce,' ³²But I say to you that every one who divorces his wife, except on the ground of unchastity, makes her an adulteress; and whoever marries a divorced woman commits adultery."

One notes that this passage is set within the larger context of the Sermon on the Mount, but more specifically within a list of teachings that demonstrates that the external requirements of the law alone will not suffice as an ethic for the people of God. These are Wisdom-type sayings spiced with a healthy dash of hyperbole (teaching by exaggeration, compare especially Matt. 5:29-30).

The saying contained in 5:32 has been the subject of much discussion. The teaching is very similar to that found in Mark 10:11, and some commentators feel that the Markan teaching was reworked by Matthew to fit his purpose. The point of contention here is the "exception," which is not found in the Markan version. Many think that Jesus' original teaching was directed against *all divorce*, but because that ideal could not be sustained in the realities of everyday living the early church added the exception. Such an interpretation is possible, but there are other explanations that are possible as well.

In Mark's account it was argued that the background for that saying lay in the historical incident that involved Herodias' leaving her husband to marry her husband's half brother. The restriction that incident evoked was expanded to apply to both husbands and wives. In Matthew 5:32, however, it appears that the discussion is strictly upon the question of divorce as a general matter of practice. Jesus, as already noted, appears to have been an advocate of monogamy and the sanctity of marriage. Therefore, this teaching should be understood against that setting. It is interesting to note once again that Jesus does not say that divorce is wrong; here he argues that divorce should not be exercised except for the most serious matters. Anyone who divorces his wife for whim must understand that he is placing his wife, innocent of any real offense, in a situation where she will be forced into a situation of sinfulness (perhaps as a second wife). Further, whoever marries the divorced woman (as a second wife) is violating the basic teaching of Jesus about marriage, that is *one* man and *one* woman. In that society almost any woman was dependent on a male for security and support. If she were set out, this would place her in a position where she would be forced to "commit adultery." Jesus is speaking here, probably in hyperbole, to emphasize the serious nature of divorce.

The "exception" clause then points out the grounds for such an extreme action. Most traditions render the Greek word *porneia* as either "adultery" or "unchastity," and those are certainly two quite legitimate meanings of the word. In the Judaism of the first century, however, the word *porneia* had a much wider range of meaning. It could refer to incestuous relationships, illicit marriages, cultic prostitution, disloyalty (in a more general sense), inordinate love of money, pride, wrong worship practices, injustice, or simply doing evil to someone else! To limit the meaning of the word strictly to sexual immorality of some sort may be far too rigid an interpretation and may well limit the original meaning of the saying.

There are several points to be noted about this passage. The most important is that the saying is incorporated into a long series of sayings designed to show that the external requirements of the law are not the most important aspects of the law. The deeper meaning and interest of the law are much more important than the superficial legalisms that were often used in improper ways. If indeed rigid adherence to the letter of the law was not to be a part of the new community of Christians, it becomes apparent that whatever else the saying may mean, it cannot and should not be used as the basis for a new legalism dealing with marriage and divorce.

The emphasis, as in Mark, is placed on the serious nature of marriage. This relationship is important because it has implications and ramifications far beyond the two people involved. For this reason the person who has the right of divorce must not use this part of the law for personal whims nor capricious actions. If one understands the passage in this manner, the debate about whether the early church altered Jesus' saying because they felt it too unreasonable becomes irrelevant. That argument is based upon a wrongly held legalistic understanding of Jesus' teaching in Mark 10:2-9, which Jesus did not

intend *and the early church did not interpret as a legalism.*
Divorce is not forbidden—but it is surely dis-
couraged. The emphasis again is upon the importance and significance of marriage.

> *Matthew 19:3-9:* ³And Pharisees came up to him and
> tested him by asking, "Is it lawful to divorce one's
> wife for any cause?" ⁴He answered, "Have you not
> read that he who made them from the beginning
> made them male and female, ⁵and said, 'For this
> reason a man shall leave his father and mother and
> be joined to his wife, and the two shall become one
> flesh'? ⁶So they are no longer two but one flesh. What
> therefore God has joined together, let not man put
> asunder." ⁷They said to him, "Why then did Moses
> command one to give a certificate of divorce, and to
> put her away?" ⁸He said to them, "For your hardness
> of heart Moses allowed you to divorce your wives, but
> from the beginning it was not so. ⁹And I say to you:
> whoever divorces his wife, except for unchastity, and
> marries another, commits adultery."

This episode incorporated into Matthew's Gospel
appears to be a different version of the incident
related in Mark 10:2-9. The setting is much the same
in that the Pharisees question Jesus in order to "test"
him. The arrangement is somewhat different, and
the question has an addition to it, ". . . for any cause."
It is interesting to note that the Greek can be
translated "every cause," which could carry a slightly
different nuance. The appropriate meaning may be

more easily ascertained after examining the entire section, however.

The question obviously reflects the ongoing debate among the Rabbinic groups with regard to the meaning of Deuteronomy 24:1 and the attempt to define "some indecency." Jesus turns the discussion (as in Mark) away from an emphasis upon how to get out of marriage to an emphasis upon what real marriage ought to be. In Matthew's account, however, the Pharisees begin to argue, asking why Moses even allowed divorce. The response was that divorce was allowed because of human frailty and sinfulness. It is never said that the law had been superseded, but the clear direction of Jesus' comments pointed in the direction of real marriage, one man and one woman becoming one entity together, and away from the practice of divorce based on whim or flimsy reasonings.

If one reads the text carefully, the teaching of this passage appears to be directed not against divorce *per se* but against the practice of divorcing one's wife for no good cause. There is a stern warning to the husband who would act in such an irresponsible way. This is emphasized in two ways. First, the "exception" clause is again found here in Matthew's Gospel. This "exception," designated again under the word *porneia,* probably included any significant act of unfaithfulness, sexual or otherwise (compare above, pp. 57-58, for the many different possibilities of meaning for *porneia*), but the intent of the saying is to demonstrate that divorce must be based on significant grounds to be legitimate.

The second way in which the husband is warned about frivolously sending away his wife lies in the comment in verse 9. The interpreter again finds a problem in the transmission of the text in that there are at least four possible readings for this passage in the Greek. Without going into tedious detail suffice it to say that the majority of the ancient texts read something like this: "Whoever dismisses his wife except for unchastity *(porneia) makes her commit adultery*" (italics mine). If this is the closest to the original saying, then the passage places upon the husband (who divorces his wife for frivolous reasons) the responsibility for the moral life of the woman. The assumption could presumably have been that the divorced woman would then have had to become a second wife for someone (or perhaps worse), and that sin was the responsibility of the divorcing husband. Again one sees the strong insistence of Jesus upon monogamy and the serious nature of the marriage covenant.

One can see that Jesus is not specifying laws to be followed to the letter; he is responding to questions put to him by the religious authorities. The key phrase here is "for *any* [or every] cause." The answer to that question is that "any [or every] cause" should not be considered adequate for the dissolution of a relationship so sacred to God. There is no direct denial here, however, that the old law dealing with divorce has been nullified, and it is clear from the "exception" clause that divorce is allowable if the situation is serious enough to warrant that course of action.

One final comment perhaps is in order. There does not seem to be in this passage any teaching that a woman who has been wrongfully "put away" is involved in any immorality if and when she shall remarry. Any sin that may be involved lies on the head of the irresponsible and frivolous husband who has divorced her without just cause.

> *Matthew 19:10-12:* ¹⁰The disciples said to him, "If such is the case of a man with his wife, it is not expedient to marry." ¹¹But he said to them, "Not all men can receive this saying, but only those to whom it is given. ¹²For there are eunuchs who have been so from birth, and there are eunuchs who have been made eunuchs by men, and there are eunuchs who have made themselves eunuchs for the sake of the kingdom of heaven. He who is able to receive this, let him receive it."

Most scholars feel that this passage originally had no connection with either Jesus' teaching on marriage and divorce or this particular occasion in Jesus' ministry. The thought is that Matthew has added the saying at this point by "catchword" or by similarity of content. This may be correct, but the way Matthew has welded the units together in his narrative account certainly makes the two speak to much the same issue.

The disciples here are made to appear very much a part of their world and its value system. If indeed marriage is such a serious matter and divorce can only be allowed for the most serious of offenses, why bother to marry at all?! The basic idea in the teaching of Jesus at this point seems to be that the requirements of the new life of the Kingdom are, indeed, difficult. Becoming a part of the new Kingdom of God is never an easy matter. It requires total commitment to God's ways, not the ways of the world. To many of the people of that time marriage and divorce were viewed in a cavalier fashion, but those who have become part of God's new Kingdom know that this relationship is special both for human beings and in the plan and purpose of God.

In reality this passage has nothing to say about divorce and simply reiterates the principle that marriage is a most serious relationship. This Wisdom-hyperbole saying seems to be more directed toward the commitment one makes when becoming a member of the new Kingdom. If the teaching has anything directly to say about marriage or divorce, the principle is that there may be certain occupations where it would be best for a person not to be married. For example, early Christian preachers traveled over the Greco-Roman world. To sustain a wife and family under such circumstances was very difficult. In fact, most would have to be absent from their homes for long periods of time. In such a situation where such a life-style was accepted, marriage and family had to take a secondary position, and in such a setting marriage, as Jesus described it, would be impossible. (One is reminded of Paul's own comment about being single in I Cor. 7:7-8, and his comments about others who took their wives along in their evangelizing work, I Cor. 9:3-5.)

> *Luke 16:18:* Every one who divorces his wife and marries another commits adultery, and he who marries a woman divorced from her husband commits adultery.

This Lucan passage is somewhat more difficult to understand than those previously discussed because the saying is not part of a longer story or precise setting. The larger context for this saying in Luke's arrangement consists of a collection of teachings aimed directly at the religious authorities. In 15:1 the setting Luke gives for the three parables of things "lost" (the lost sheep, the lost coin, and the *two* lost sons) begins with the Pharisees and the scribes being offended because Jesus is eating with "sinners." In 16:14-15 Luke reiterates that it is against the Pharisees that Jesus is speaking. The saying about divorce, then, is set within that broader context, but there is really no narrative connection to set the teaching more precisely.

One notes that in this saying there is no reciprocal interpretation of the teaching in the light of a new setting (as Mark 10:10-12, where in Roman society the woman may have the right of divorce). Neither is there an "exception" clause such as was found in both of the Matthean passages, nor is there any reference to the "certificate of divorce." Because of these factors many scholars believe that this saying in Luke is as close to the original teaching of Jesus as can be obtained.

It is true that the saying as it stands here seems to be "untampered" with. No saying, however, has any real meaning unless it is placed within a context of some kind. If Luke, therefore, intended for the reader to assume a context of conflict with the religious authorities (as Mark and Matthew have), then the saying would have essentially the same meaning here as it did in those two Gospels.

If Luke, however, did not intend the reader to understand the saying in that type of context, what did he intend? Some have argued that this may have been the saying originally directed against Herod for marrying the wife of his half brother (perhaps without benefit of divorce). Those who understand the teaching in this way refer to Luke 16:16-17. In these verses there are references to John the Baptizer, the preaching of the Kingdom of God, and violence of some sort. All of these would certainly fit the historical setting of John's ministry and his death relating to his outspoken denunciation of the marriage of Herod and Herodias.

A third interpretation should be familiar by now. Some hold that the saying as it stands here has nothing to do with marriage and divorce *per se,* but they see in this a clear warning against polygyny. This saying then would presuppose Jesus' strong emphasis upon monogamy and his strong denunciation against divorce for frivolous matters. The teaching (found elsewhere) is that whoever divorces his wife for less than the most valid of reasons brings upon himself guilt for what he has done and any guilt of the divorced wife.

What this investigation demonstrates, therefore, is that even with Luke's citation of a seemingly simple and clear-cut saying of Jesus, there is uncertainty as to its precise and exact meaning. The statement cannot be used, therefore, as an absolute legalistic teaching about divorce as some have argued. The background and setting seem to point to a meaning quite similar to that found in Mark and Matthew.

Summary of Jesus' Teachings

Having examined all of the sayings on divorce and marriage contained in the Gospels, we can now draw from them some understanding of what Jesus taught about these subjects and how the church has interpreted and used what Jesus said.

It is crystal clear that Jesus and the early church understood marriage as a God-given gift for the beautification of life for both individuals and society as a whole. The structure of society, especially the new society of God's people, finds its stability and order in the strong family unit. Jesus interpreted the Creation stories in this way. Marriage is defined as two persons becoming one, obviously in a monogamous relationship. Where that happens *there is no possibility of divorce.* The question for the church today is whether there is a real marriage if this growing together does not take place. Can one call two persons cohabitating, even legally, "married"? There are some who would understand marriage in such a legalistic way, but there are others who see such a situation more as a "legalized adultery" sanctioned by society and the state. Such a situation can be sanctioned by the state. Can the church sanction such a situation? Should it? Whatever one's answers to these questions, it is clear that Jesus viewed marriage as a serious and significant human relationship, the importance of which may be second only to one's relationship with God.

From the examination of these sayings of Jesus on this topic one primary consideration seems to continue to be fundamental for a correct understanding of the teachings. That is the historical context that served as the setting for Jesus' teaching in these areas. It seems clear, especially from Mark and Matthew (perhaps even from Luke), that the debate about divorce and on what grounds divorce could or should be granted, which was going on between the Rabbinic schools, was a significant part of the background for Jesus' comments. In Mark and Matthew the setting is that of a question put to Jesus by the Pharisees and scribes; in Luke the saying is set within the broader context of teaching directed against the religious leaders. To interpret these teachings properly one must always keep this situation in mind.

A second background component for one or more of Jesus' teachings is quite probably to be found in the situation concerning Herod and his half brother's wife. This relationship was not only considered incestuous, but Herodias may not even have been divorced from her first husband. The restriction against leaving a husband or wife and marrying another may well have had this specific incident as its model, which is quite different from a situation where people are properly divorced and remarry.

Further, one must remember that divorced women often had to remarry as second wives or even become concubines to survive in that period. This was especially contrary to Jesus' insistence on monogamy and placed the women in serious straits with regard to moral and ethical considerations for members of the new Kingdom. Jesus' teaching was directed at those husbands who divorced their wives for less than substantial reasons.

What is beginning to emerge from this study thus far are some broad principles or guidelines that can be applied in various situations. This does not mean that these principles or guidelines will be easy to understand or to apply in every context. Far from it! But there are some ideas that are beginning to crystalize. It would be best, however, to examine the remainder of the New Testament teaching in these matters before drawing all of them together in some sort of logical pattern.

The Teaching of Paul

I Corinthians 7

Now concerning the matters about which you wrote. It is well for a man not to touch a woman. ²But because of the temptation to immorality, each man should have his own wife and each woman her own husband. ³The husband should give to his wife her conjugal rights, and likewise the wife to her husband. ⁴For the wife does not rule over her own body, but the husband does; likewise the husband does not rule over his own body, but the wife does. ⁵Do not refuse one another except perhaps by agreement for a season, that you may devote yourselves to prayer; but then come together again, lest Satan tempt you through lack of self-control. ⁶I say this by way of concession, not of command. ⁷I wish that all were as I myself am. But each has his own special gift from God, one of one kind and one of another.

⁸To the unmarried and the widows I say that it is well for them to remain single as I do. ⁹But if they cannot exercise self-control, they should marry. For it is better to marry than to be aflame with passion.

¹⁰To the married I give charge, not I but the Lord, that the wife should not separate from her husband ¹¹(but if she does, let her remain single or else be reconciled to her husband)—and that the husband should not divorce his wife.

¹²To the rest I say, not the Lord, that if any brother has a wife who is an unbeliever, and she consents to live with him, he should not divorce her. ¹³If any woman has a husband who is an unbeliever, and he consents to live with her, she should not divorce him. ¹⁴For the unbelieving husband is consecrated through his wife, and the unbelieving wife is consecrated through her husband. Otherwise, your children would be unclean, but as it is they are holy. ¹⁵But if the unbelieving partner desires to separate, let it be so; in such a case the brother or sister is not

bound. For God has called us to peace. [16]Wife, how do you know whether you will save your husband? Husband, how do you know whether you will save your wife?

[17]Only, let every one lead the life which the Lord has assigned to him, and in which God has called him. This is my rule in all the churches. [18]Was any one at the time of his call already circumcised? Let him not seek to remove the marks of circumcision. Was any one at the time of his call uncircumcised? Let him not seek circumcision. [19]For neither circumcision counts for anything nor uncircumcision, but keeping the commandments of God. [20]Every one should remain in the state in which he was called. [21]Were you a slave when called? Never mind. But if you can gain your freedom, avail yourself of the opportunity. [22]For he who was called in the Lord as a slave is a freedman of the Lord. Likewise he who was free when called is a slave of Christ. [23]You were bought with a price; do not become slaves of men. [24]So, brethren, in whatever state each was called, there let him remain with God.

[25]Now concerning the unmarried, I have no command of the Lord, but I give my opinion as one who by the Lord's mercy is trustworthy. [26]I think that in view of the present distress it is well for a person to remain as he is. [27]Are you bound to a wife? Do not seek to be free. Are you free from a wife? Do not seek marriage. [28]But if you marry, you do not sin, and if a girl marries she does not sin. Yet those who marry will have worldly troubles, and I would spare you that. [29]I mean, brethren, the appointed time has grown very short; from now on, let those who have wives live as though they had none, [30]and those who

mourn as though they were not mourning, and those who rejoice as though they were not rejoicing, and those who buy as though they had no goods, [31]and those who deal with the world as though they had no dealings with it. For the form of this world is passing away.

[32]I want you to be free from anxieties. The unmarried man is anxious about the affairs of the Lord, how to please the Lord; [33]but the married man is anxious about worldly affairs, how to please his wife, [34]and his interests are divided. And the unmarried woman or girl is anxious about the affairs of the Lord, how to be holy in body and spirit; but the married woman is anxious about worldly affairs, how to please her husband. [35]I say this for your own benefit, not to lay any restraint upon you, but to promote good order and to secure your undivided devotion to the Lord.

[36]If any one thinks that he is not behaving properly toward his betrothed, if his passions are strong, and it has to be, let him do as he wishes: let them marry—it is no sin. [37]But whoever is firmly established in his heart, being under no necessity but having his desire under control, and has determined this in his heart, to keep her as his betrothed, he will do well. [38]So that he who marries his betrothed does well; and he who refrains from marriage will do better.

[39]A wife is bound to her husband as long as he lives. If the husband dies, she is free to be married to whom she wishes, only in the Lord. [40]But in my judgment she is happier if she remains as she is. And I think that I have the Spirit of God.

Paul's teaching on marriage and divorce is found basically in one of his letters to the Corinthian church known to us as I Corinthians. This letter deals with a host of problems being encountered in the church at Corinth. Paul attempted to speak to those problems as best he could. Some came to his attention by word of mouth (through Chloe's people, I Cor. 1:11) and some by letter from the people in Corinth (compare I Cor. 7:1).

The matters Paul discusses in chapter 7 deal basically with two issues. One is the question of whether sexual intercourse is in itself sinful. Some persons in the church at Corinth were evidently arguing that this was so. These people were basically influenced by the Greek idea that the flesh and material things are sinful because they belong to this world. A truly "spiritual" person does not participate in anything fleshly or physical because such activities are inherently evil. Sex, because it is at least partially expressed through the contact of flesh with flesh, is therefore sinful and should be banned from the Christian's life. Thus the argument seems to have run. This was one problem.

Another item of debate seems to have been partially at least related to the first point. Should Christians marry, stay married, or separate? Since marriage involves sexual activity, should not a Christian abstain from marriage?

Paul spoke to these issues and more. First, he argued that there is nothing immoral about sexual intercourse provided that it is performed within the proper context. To him the proper context was the marriage covenant. He made it clear that within this context the wife and the husband *both* have conjugal rights (I Cor. 7:3-4); in fact, it is difficult to find anywhere a more "equal" statement about marriage than these verses!

Some persons in the Corinthian church were arguing that even if persons were married they should agree to abstain from sexual relations. Paul, knowing the innate drive to procreate, which is built into all of nature's creatures (even humans), argued that persons who were in the married state remain therein and "not refuse" each other except for a short period of time by mutual consent. He then *commanded* them to come back together so that temptation would not cause them to behave immorally in this matter. The "concession" in this passage is to those who wanted to abstain for a period of time not the concession of their coming back together (as some have misunderstood the passage).

The next problem in this area concerns those who are unmarried or widowed. Should these persons remarry? The answer Paul gives is that it is best for them to remain unmarried. If, however, their natural sexual desires are extremely strong, it is better to marry rather than risk acting in an unseemly manner and thereby causing their witness to Christ and for the church to be tainted. His argument here is not based on the assumption that sexual relationships in marriage is wrong. Rather Paul believed that Jesus would return in the very near future. This belief he held in common with the early church in general. The idea was that Jesus would return soon to consummate the Kingdom of God, which had been inaugurated in his ministry. Before the *Parousia* (the technical term for Jesus' return), there would occur a period wherein the early Christians would experience a time of persecution. This persecution was to be extremely intense. Thus it would be very difficult for persons to be responsible for themselves, let alone wives or husbands or even small children. Because of such a belief Paul counseled the people in Corinth to remain unmarried not because it was evil to marry or an inferior life-style but because of practical considerations (compare especially I Cor. 7:8, 25-28, 32-38).

Paul emphasized that sexual relationships within the proper context were quite proper. His Jewish heritage caused him to exalt the marriage covenant because such an institution was viewed as a gift of God for the enjoyment and betterment of individuals and society. Order and proper decorum, however, had to be part of the Christian's life-style. Even in those "last times of impending distress," the counsel not to marry was not given as an absolute but as a practical consideration. This is not an absolute principle for every time and every place, but there could be analogous times and circumstances when the teaching of Paul in this context might again be considered as practical and worthy of heed.

In I Corinthians 7:10-11 Paul continues to speak to the issue of wives and husbands who feel that they should abstain from sexual contact. In this instance the situation is somewhat different from that mentioned previously of married couples living together with the agreement to abstain from sexual activity. Here the situation has reached the point where the two have agreed to separate or even perhaps divorce. Paul urges them in the authority of Jesus' teaching to remain married, not to separate or divorce over ideas that were ultimately trivial or on grounds that were misunderstood. Again the Greek words that are translated "separate" and "divorce" may have the simpler connotation of "leaving." If anyone did separate for this purpose, however, it was understood that if they began sexual activity again that it must be with the original wife or husband.

It is at this point that Paul specifically turns to the problem of divorce (I Cor. 7:12-16). The question put to him was whether someone who was already married and who had later become a Christian could continue to live with a person who was not and had not become a Christian. Paul's advice for such persons was to remain married if the unbelieving partner was willing to continue the relationship. If the unbelieving partner wished to separate, Paul argues that such is acceptable if not preferable! The comment, "God has called us to [that is, for the state of] peace," shows that Paul considered the well-being (the essential meaning of "peace") of the persons to supersede the simple "staying together to save the marriage." It is interesting that Paul could condone and even suggest that separation was acceptable even though he obviously knew Jesus' comment about marriage and divorce (compare I Cor. 7:10). The principle involved here is that there may be certain marital situations that are unsuitable for the well-being of the people involved, and in such instances these relationships can and should be dissolved.

One possible consequence of such a situation is not discussed by Paul, however. That is, in such a case where the nonbeliever wishes to separate and divorce, is it acceptable for the Christian partner to remarry? The commentators are quite divided over this point. Some argue that Paul's teaching to remain single in verse 11 is still valid even in this new and different context. Still others argue that Paul's overall advice is not to marry if one is single because of the "impending distress" (that is, the *Parousia*). These two groups, therefore, argue that Paul would not allow remarriage for persons in such a situation. These interpreters believe that the injunction in verse 39 (I Cor. 7), which specifically relates to the death of a marriage partner, is a specific rule applicable to all situations. That is, no person, once married, can ever marry again unless and until the first partner has died. Only then is the privilege of remarriage available to the Christian.

Others, however, point to the comments of Paul basically presented in I Corinthians 7:9, 29, and 39. In each of these cases there is no stipulation against marriage, and thus these interpreters feel that Paul definitely would allow remarriage for someone in the situation described in verse 15. The only condition would be that such a person should marry another Christian (compare v. 39).

As with the sayings of Jesus on this topic, Paul's teaching here is not as easy to understand as some have thought. We do not know the specific context to which Paul was speaking so that some of the subtleties of the argument may be lost to us. There are a few points of interest here, however, which are obvious even beyond the complexities of understanding all the specifics of the instructions to the people of Corinth.

Paul accepted as genuine the teaching of Jesus that marriage basically is for life. But it is interesting to note that he does not understand this teaching to be an absolute legalistic commandment that can never be broken. He allows for separation and divorce in certain instances (compare I Cor. 7:10-11, 15). In the former he seems to say that there is to be no "marriage" except with the initial marriage partner, but the situation here addressed in fact related to the sexual abstinence question with which Paul had attempted to deal and which seems to have been a major point of contention among the church members at Corinth (compare vv. 1-9). The comments then of verses 10-11 flow smoothly from that discussion, and these are not really directed toward divorce but separation over other matters.

In the latter situation, divorce is directly addressed and Paul seems to think that divorce is certainly the lesser of the "evils" involved. It is better to be separate and divorced (even though the Christian is under obligation to do all she/he can to make the marriage work) than to live in a situation where the "peace" (well-being) of all is endangered.

All of this, it should be remembered, is set within the context of Paul's own belief that the return of Christ would take place very soon, within his lifetime. It may be interesting indeed to know what his thoughts would have been had he not looked for an early return of Jesus but rather looked toward the future "long range." In all probability the principles and basic teachings would not have changed, but some of the implications of his thought may have been spelled out in more detail. For that we would probably be grateful since Paul is such a marvelous interpreter of the Christian life.

What About Remarriage?

There are several other passages in the New Testament that have some bearing upon marriage. While they do not really add anything of great significance to the teachings already examined, there are some interesting "side issues" that should be highlighted. One of these, of most significance for society today, concerns the problem of remarriage. If divorce does occur, what about the possibility of remarriage? Some have argued that while divorce in certain situations *may* be acceptable, the divorcee must never remarry. And if that person does remarry, adultery is being committed. Such thinking has caused much anguish to sensitive people who have divorced and remarried. The guilt has in some instances become so great that the second marriage has been harmed not because of the relationship between the two persons but because of perceived religious teachings about this situation.

What does the biblical teaching have to say about the issue of remarriage after divorce? Again, one finds certain ideas and principles that relate to this problem but very little by way of specific instruction. In the Old Testament era it appears that everyone was expected to be married. When divorce occurred, the man and the woman seemed to seek new partners. In that society the man had more options open to him than the woman. Because of that circumstance it appears that many divorced women became an additional wife for someone else. It seems that in the older period of biblical history no stigma was attached to remarriage after divorce.

In the New Testament teachings, however, subject as they are to the priority of Jesus' directions, the emphasis came to be placed on monogamous marriage. Because of this one finds the emphasis on divorce only for the most serious of problems since divorce for the woman meant that she might well be forced to be a second wife to survive in that society. The emphasis placed upon adultery after divorce appears to have a twofold purpose: (1) as an argument against polygamy, and (2) a hyperbole-type teaching to emphasize to the husband divorcing his wife for frivolous reasons that any sin the divorced wife later commits is his responsibility. If polygamy is the primary target, then single divorced persons could be assumed to have the right of remarriage.

Paul says nothing explicit about remarriage after divorce because of his understanding that the *Parousia* was about to come. His general guide for any who were unmarried was for them to remain unmarried since Jesus was to return soon. He did say, however, that if unmarried persons decided to marry that no sin was attached to that. Is the principle here broad enough to include divorced persons also? Would a divorced person be included among those designated as "unmarried"? The answer is probably "yes."

An interesting situation arose in the later New Testament period that could possibly shed some light on the matter of remarriage. The early church believed that the church itself should care for its own membership who had *no* means to support themselves (compare Acts 4:32-35; 6:1-3). Again, since they believed that the *Parousia* was about to take place soon, the matter of support for the needy was not foreseen as a pressing, long-term problem. When the *Parousia* did not materialize, however, the situation was somewhat altered. How could the working people of the church afford to support a larger number of needy persons, usually widows? And how could the church keep some more unscrupulous persons from using the church's generosity for their (undeserved) benefit? That situation had obviously gotten so far out of hand that the matter had become extremely serious by the late first century A.D.

In I Timothy 5:3-16 the author sets out rules and guidelines to assist the church in determining exactly who was and who was not a "real" widow, worthy of the church's support. The support of this group over a long period of time had become a real burden for the church, and the church is advised to "honor" only widows who were "real widows." One can read the specific qualifications in the text itself, but the important aspect of the discussion for our topic lies in the directive for all young widows to remarry. Not only were these persons a burden to the church itself, but their activities had become a source of embarrassment for the church in that community (compare 5:14). To be sure this section does not talk about divorced persons, but the principle that younger people who had been married and were presently single should remarry could possibly, perhaps even probably, be applied to divorced persons as well.

If one accepts the general idea of the biblical writers that as a rule persons are naturally more fulfilled and can make a more positive contribution to society in a family situation, it seems legitimate to conjecture that the remarriage of divorced persons is not only permissible but perhaps desirable.

CHAPTER III

Some Observations About Marriage and Divorce According to the Biblical Teachings

As the Apostle Paul said on occasion, "What therefore shall we say about these things?" Having examined the biblical passages dealing with marriage and divorce, the interpreter must make some connections between the principles and guidelines of the Scripture and the problems in present-day society. That we live in a society where divorce is constantly mounting in terms of numbers of people involved and that the religious community is trying to make sense of the situation go without saying. The question becomes how to take those teachings of the Scripture and apply them to society and individual lives today. This task is not an easy one to fulfill.

It is obvious that our society today is not the same, culturally speaking, as that from which the biblical writers and writings came. Things were far more simple, far less complex, and "roles" for men and women, husbands and wives were quite well defined in that peiod of history. Persons were expected to fit into these roles, and by and large they did.

Contrast that rather immobile, static society with ours, and the diversity of the one from the other is very great indeed. We live in a complex, modern world, with far more freedom for both men and women and, therefore, far more responsibilities (or at least pressures). Even though role models for husbands and wives in our society have been in the past fairly "set" in traditional forms, those stereotypes are today rapidly disintegrating. Women, rightly so, are being allowed to become first-class citizens after all these centuries. But that is to digress from our basic point.

The question that conscientious Christian people are asking is: What does the Christian Scripture teach about marriage and divorce? And how can that teaching speak to us in our own particular setting with its own problems and difficulties? The answers to those questions are not as simple and clear cut as some have thought.

The biblical passages dealing with the topics of divorce and marriage have been examined, albeit briefly, but one can determine that they are not as simple to understand as we might like! Several points, however, do seem to emerge from those passages. The most important emphasis is that marriage is a positive, God-given, even foundational gift to individuals and to society. Its potential for good in life is indeed far reaching. Next to one's relationship with God, the relationship of a man and a woman within the marriage bond seems perhaps to be potentially the most important and significant of all human relationships.

From the beginning, Jesus said, God intended that the man the woman should become *one*. There could be no more beautiful definition of marriage ever given. Where that kind of relationship exists, *there is no possibility of divorce*. Even to think such a thing is illogical and contradictory. God intended that marriage be permanent and lasting, for in marriage there is a covenant of commitment that is accepted on the part of each person. The marriage relationship is intended to be mutually supportive for each of the persons involved.

Marriage was considered such a potential source of hope that in biblical times the moment of marriage was viewed as a most joyous event. Several of Jesus' parables and incidents in his life centered in the joy and happiness and hope that surrounds this momentous occasion in a person's life. Marriage is important, however, not only because of what it means to individuals but for what it means to society. It potentially gives to the community a strong basis for the continuation of that society, an order and structure for life both individually and collectively, and it provides the family as the institution that is basically responsible for morals, ethics, and religion—those matters that give life value and quality.

There is no question, therefore, that the biblical teachings understand that marriage is to be between one man and one woman. There seem to be several reasons for this, not the least of which is that marriage is one means of regulating human sexuality. Human sexuality is viewed by the biblical writers as a gift from God for the continuation and enjoyment of the human race. This sexuality, however, must be properly channeled because of the intense innate sexual drive that humans have as part of the natural order and the human propensity toward sin and rebellion—the human tendency to debase anything and everything. The biblical writers, therefore, understand the appropriate location for human sexuality to be in a context of commitment and loyalty, which is found primarily within the marriage covenant. This understanding presupposes the total commitment of each person to the other, and this commitment is to issue in a transforming relationship for both individuals, which transcends mere sexuality. This relationship was understood, ideally at least, as an intimate and significant process whereby two people somehow become one. This is the great mystery of marriage, how two individuals can become one while yet remaining two, how two people can be one while still retaining their individuality and even having that individuality increased and heightened.

The marriage relationship was held in such high esteem that the New Testament writer of Ephesians used it as an analogy for the relationship between Christ and the church. How can a person become one with Christ and the other members of the Christian fellowship and still retain one's individuality? In fact, have that individuality heightened rather than submerged? It is a mystery and yet it is a simple mystery. In a relationship of total commitment and trust, where each party pledges to work for the betterment of the other *first*, the environment for growth and development is established, which provides the ultimate opportunity for the positive development of each party within the covenant agreement. The ideal promises great dividends both for individuals and society.

But alas, this ideal for marriage is similar to all of the other ideal principles and guidelines given for Christian living. Unfortunately, we do not yet fully live in the kingdom of God. Jesus looked forward to a time when the kingdom would be fulfilled; Paul taught that Christians, even though they were already a part of the new age, nevertheless still lived under the old age with its ambiguities and evil influences. Even the great author of the Gospel of John, while emphasizing that the Christian has been raised to a new quality and level of life, still recognized that Christians live in "this world," which is opposed to the values and standards of God.

It appears from a detailed study of the New Testament passages, therefore, that while marriage is considered permanent and is ideally to be permanent, there are certain guidelines by which to measure *real* marriage. The harsh realities of this world raise the fundamental question: What does one do when there is no *real* marriage? What happens when the two do not become one? And in this world such occasions do arise! From the study of the biblical passages it seems clear that it is assumed that there are situations where "divorce" (if that is the proper word) can and *perhaps should* be sanctioned.

Jesus' teaching was primarily directed toward the ideal of what marriage was supposed to be. The historical circumstances and the background out of which he answered questions about marriage and divorce must be taken into account when trying to determine what he really said and meant. Another question is also in order: Did Jesus intend his sayings to be taken literally as a "legal bond" for every situation? It would seem that such a legalistic and absolute understanding of this set of teachings about marriage would be quite out of line with the way one properly interprets the biblical materials.

So many, including official interpreters, have taken for granted for so long that Jesus and the New Testament writers denied *all divorce* that the New Testament passages have not really been examined carefully to ascertain what was actually said and meant. It is also an interesting phenomenon to see passages taken from Jesus' teaching and Paul's letters used in such an absolute and legalistic manner. That is a curious situation. For here were two persons who were above all else opposed to legalism, but some have made their teachings into a new legalism, at least in the areas of marriage and divorce. If one examines carefully the teachings of Jesus and Paul on the topics of marriage and divorce, one finds several emphases. There is in both the primary concern for the positive and lasting relationship that comes from the marriage covenant. But also in the teaching of both there are clearly points at which divorce seems to be a real and viable option—even for the most dedicated Christian. As Paul said, "God has called us to well-being." It is also an interesting point that even though Paul knew Jesus' teaching about marriage and divorce, he did not interpret it literally or legalistically! The process of making a legalism of such sayings came later than Paul.

Having said this, however, the present writer wants to make it clear that divorce, while assumed to be legitimate by the biblical teachings, is to be considered a very serious matter. This is true because of the very significant nature of marriage, which divorce (at least legally) destroys. Divorce is failure; divorce is, to a certain degree, sin. There should be no mistake about that. But is it always the greatest sin? *The* sin from which there is no forgiveness or relief? If the New Testament teachings about forgiveness and new life and new beginnings and true change within people have any validity, is divorce not also to be considered under these principles?

One hears the argument today from many quarters that our problem lies in the fact that divorce is "too easy." This, they argue, is the reason for the rising rate of divorce. Having done considerable marriage counseling over the past twenty-five years, the present writer has found that charge to be almost totally *untrue*! It is very difficult to "get a divorce." Aside from the fact that this means a relationship so intimate and with such promise for good has "gone sour," there are the other factors. What legal steps have to be taken? What kind of *fair* disposition of property can be accomplished? What about children, and how will this affect them? With women especially (but also males to a certain degree), what kind of economic security can one have, especially in a society that far too often exploits women on the remunerative side of the pay scales? What about my friends and my family? What will they think? What about my job? Will I be fired? Will I now have to face the probability that unscrupulous people will take me for an "easy mark"? *NO!* Divorce is not easy.

If the church wishes to do something to assist in dealing with the alarming rise in the divorce rate, it should approach the situation from the same viewpoint as the biblical teachings—with an emphasis on the importance and the serious nature of marriage. Premarital counseling is a step in the right direction, but the counseling a couple receives in those settings is at best only superficial. A minister may know that this couple is not suited for each other (and may even refuse to marry them), but that is not going to stop the couple from getting married. They are "in love" and are determined that love conquers all problems. If the minister does not marry them, someone else will. As already noted, it is really not easy to get a divorce; what is wrong is that *it is too easy to get married* in the first place! All the premarital counseling in the world will probably not make a dent in the divorce rate.

What is needed and may help could be a program that emphasizes marital counseling in the first two or three years of marriage. Here is where the problems arise, the disappointments appear, and the realities become known. Perhaps more marriages are made or broken in the first few years of the relationship than at any other period. Counseling during this crucial time would be of much more value to the couple than all the premarital counseling one could impose before the marriage. It is in the first months that the relationship is begun that will begin the process of leading them together into "one" or in leading them apart and thus away from what real marriage is supposed to be. The development of such a program deserves the attention of the church in this very important area of human relationships.

Further, if divorce should occur, and it is certainly a trend of the times, the church should offer to the persons involved in this tragedy as much counsel, love, and attention as possible. The trauma of a broken family relationship, especially marriage, can be devastating to some people. It should be the role of the church to be an instrument of healing and redemption in such a situation. It should not be the role of the church to point accusing fingers of condemnation (even if they may be deserved). The church perhaps loses more members because of the stigma that it and some members attach to divorce than for almost any other reason. The church could and should develop strong programs for "singles," the majority of whom will be divorced persons in our present society. Too many divorced persons who are deeply religious do not feel that there is a place for them in the church. This ought not to be.

Perhaps one final comment could be presented for the purpose of discussion. After a thorough investigation of the biblical texts regarding marriage and divorce, it seems clear that making legalistic and absolute rules about this intimate human relationship is illegitimate. There is no legalism that can mandate the making of two people one. Nevertheless, there still are those who will seriously understand the biblical teaching to be: *there can be only one marriage; there cannot be any divorce.* The idea is that divorce is evil, and remarriage is simply unthinkable. If we lived in the kingdom of God, that would be true.

It is interesting that sin is understood to be a part of the life of even the best Christian people, and we allow for forgiveness for sins. The traditional view of forgiveness is found in that beloved story of Jesus and the adulterous woman, "Go and sin no more." Why is it then that the church has been so long in recognizing that people can sin and destroy marriages as easily as sinning in any other area of life? Or even if there is no gross sinning involved that people do make mistakes, and that these mistakes are made not only in the selection of a vocation or where one goes to college or where one lives, etc., but also at times in the selection of a marriage partner? It is much more tragic when a mistake is made in this area because of the more intimate nature of the relationship and because of the potential for good and for joy that is always the hope at the beginning of a marriage. But can we as human beings, who still live at least in part in the "old age," allow for mistakes and for sin and forgiveness in every area of life *except in marriage?* This really does seem to create a new legalism, and as has been pointed out Jesus and Paul especially denounced legalistic attitudes and viewpoints.

Some argue, however, that the teachings about marriage must be taken literally or all moral standards become "relative." One does not have to "relativize" everything in the world, however, to abstain from being a legalist. There are some absolute values in this world and within the Christian faith. But all of these are set within the broader context of a fallen world and within the Christian community at least of a concern for and caring about the peace, that is, well-being, of each person. Such values, therefore, are set within the context of a genuine love for and forgiveness of people who sin or who make mistakes. This does not mean that sin is condoned or that society should encourage cavalierly the making of mistakes in such an important institution as marriage, especially when marriage is unerstood as one of the stabilizing pillars of society. It does mean, however, that in this world one has to be realistic and recognize that there may be situations where divorce is the lesser of the "evils" to be chosen, where the well-being of both the parents and the children is enhanced by divorce, and where, by the grace of God, all parties involved will now have a chance at happiness and a good life. Is it really

Christian to deny people in such situations relief from the pressures of their "mistake"? Is it really Christian to demand that they (and their children) be forever miserable?

The beauty of marriage and the responsibilities and commitments involved in marriage must be emphasized to young people, people contemplating marriage, the most recently married, and even "old married couples" who need to be reminded of these things occasionally. The New Testament exalts marriage and views divorce as failure. But as with other failings of the human race, by the grace of God people can be forgiven and allowed another chance to make things right.

SELECTED
BIBLIOGRAPHY

Anderson, Hugh. *The Gospel of Mark.* Grand Rapids: Wm. B. Eerdmans Publishing Co., 1976.

Barrett, Charles K. *A Commentary on the First Epistle to the Corinthians.* New York: Harper & Row, 1968.

Drescher, John and Betty. *If We Were Starting Our Marriage Again.* Nashville: Abingdon Press, 1985.

Krantzler, Mel. *Creative Divorce.* New York: Signet, 1973.

Mueller, James R. "The Temple Scroll and the Gospel Divorce Texts," in *Revue de Qumran* (38, May, 1980), pp. 247-56.

Olsen, V. Norskov. *The New Testament Logia on Divorce.* Tübingen, Germany: J. C. B. Mohr, 1971.

Rambo, Lewis R. *The Divorcing Christian.* Nashville: Abingdon Press, 1983.

Safrai, S. and Stern, M. (eds.). *The Jewish People in the First Century: Historical Geography, Political History, Social, Cultural, and Religious Life and Institutions.* 2 vols. Van Gorcum & Co.: B. V.-Assn, 1974, 1976.

Sapp, Stephen. *Sexuality, the Bible, and Science.* Philadelphia: Fortress Press, 1977.

Schweizer, Eduard. *The Good News According to Matthew,* translated by D. E. Green. Atlanta: John Knox Press, 1975.

————. *The Good News According to Mark,* translated by D. H. Madvig. Atlanta: John Knox Press, 1970.

————. *The Good News According to Luke,* translated by D. E. Green. Atlanta: John Knox Press, 1984.

Willimon, William H. *Saying Yes to Marriage.* Valley Forge, Pa.: Judson Press, 1979.